© Safoo Publications 2021

Written by Amal Al-Aride
Illustrated by Kasim Al-Janabi

Preface

We take you on the journey of the Prophet Stories that are included in the Holy Quran.

All stories included are exclusively from the Holy Quran (with references) and do not contain information that has been outsourced from any other sources such as hadiths.

All information compiled in this book has been Scholar approved to ensure that the information we present to your children is correct in view of Islamic history.

We have attempted to include as much information (that is within the Holy Quran) as possible in this book. Some Prophets have not been included as information on their stories is limited.

Contents Page

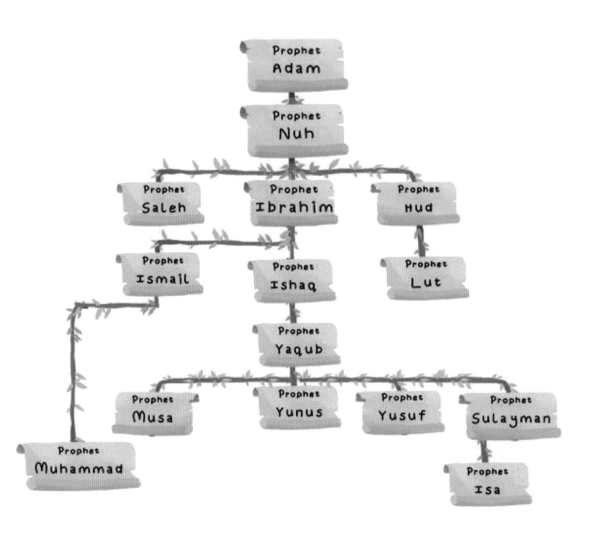

Prophets in the Quran

14 Prophet Stories Included:

Prophet Adam, Nuh, Hud, Saleh, Lut, Ibrahim, Yusuf, Musa, Sulayman, Yunus and more!

Safoo Publications

Prophet Adam

Allah created the first human being, his name was Adam and Allah always had the intention to place him on Earth.

It was a test for us all, to live in the world and show our potential, our worth.

Before Allah (the most amazing, the most high) created Prophet Adam (peace be upon him), He decided that He was going to create humans and put them on a planet called Earth. This was Allah's plan and He told the angels that this is where humans would live and have babies and look after their families.

The angels were worried and they told Allah that they thought it was better not to create humans because they will just cause trouble on Earth. They thought that angels, such as themselves were a better creation because they love Allah and are always good. Allah told them that He knows everything, He knows that which they do not know.

Holy Quran

"Allah knows what to reveal and what to conceal" (3:33)

Allah made Prophet Adam out of clay, He made the clay in the (3:59) shape of Prophet Adam and taught him the names of everything. Allah told Prophet Adam the names of all the angels and told him to show the angels what (2:31) he learnt. Allah showed the angels how smart Adam was and they were amazed by what Allah had created. Allah told the angels to bow to Prophet Adam.

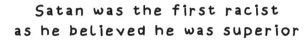

Satan was the first racist as he believed he was superior

He thought fire was better than clay

For Satan cried, "I am made of burning fire, he is earth, therefore I am higher"

(2:34) The angels listened to Allah but Iblis (Satan) didn't. Iblis thought he was better than Adam because he was made out of fire and he thought fire was better than clay. So Allah told Iblis off for being proud and thinking he was better. Allah then ordered Iblis to leave heaven and Iblis had to leave, and he was very angry.

(2:34)

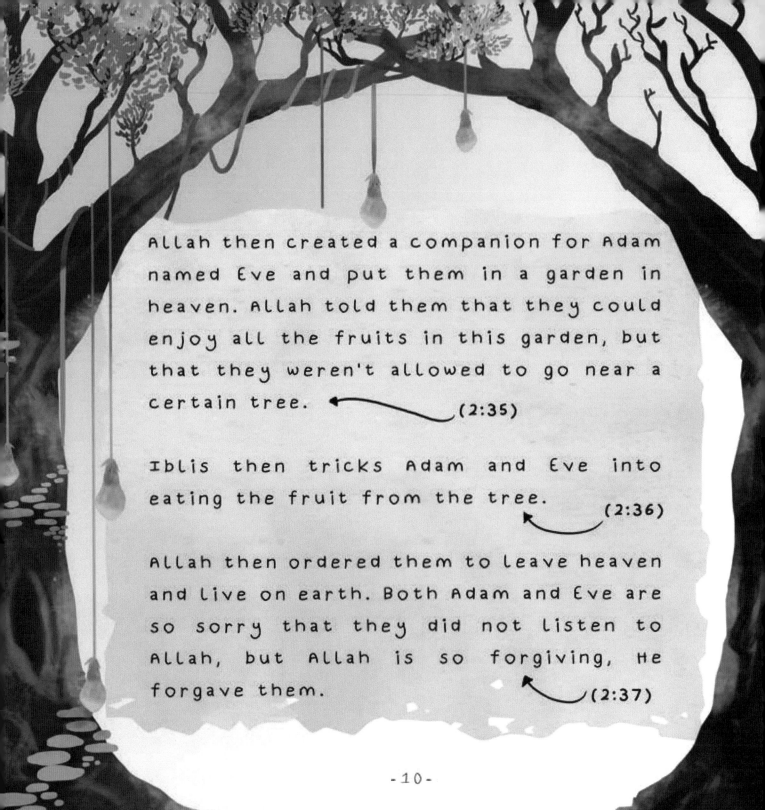

Allah then created a companion for Adam named Eve and put them in a garden in heaven. Allah told them that they could enjoy all the fruits in this garden, but that they weren't allowed to go near a certain tree. (2:35)

Iblis then tricks Adam and Eve into eating the fruit from the tree. (2:36)

Allah then ordered them to leave heaven and live on earth. Both Adam and Eve are so sorry that they did not listen to Allah, but Allah is so forgiving, He forgave them. (2:37)

And He taught Adam the names, all of them; then he presented
them to the angels, and said, "Tell Me the names of these, if you
are sincere." (2:31)

Prophet Nuh

Prophet Noah's people were slow minded, it took them a while to establish between right and wrong.

They weren't the brightest bunch, which could explain why Noah lived so long.

Prophet Nuh (peace be upon him) preached Islam and lived for at least 950 years.

He was a good man, he would always tell his people how amazing Allah was and that they should worship only Allah, instead of statues. Unfortunately, they didn't really listen to him. So Allah told Prophet Nuh that a flood would arrive.

(7:59)

Holy Quran

"We sent Nuh to his people, and he remained with them a thousand years minus fifty years..." (29:14)

Allah also told Prophet Nuh that he needed to build a ship and put two of every animal on board, as well some of his followers who believed in him. (11:35-41)

It took Prophet Nuh a while to build the ship, and people at the time who didn't believe him would make fun of him, they called him crazy, they would say "what kind of person would build a ship with no river or sea near by?" (7:62)

For the time had come for a natural disaster,
issued by Allah, the one and only master.

The waves they came like mountains,
they gushed like endless fountains.

The flood finally came when Prophet Nuh finished building the ship. Even when the flood came Noah's people still did not believe him and all those people drowned, this included one of Prophet Nuh's sons.

(7:64)

"And construct the ship under Our Eyes and with Our Inspiration and address Me not on behalf of those who did wrong; they are surely to be drowned." (11:37)

Prophet Hud

A great gust of wind, through the city it did blow,
Allah sent a punishment and it was a tornado.

(26:128—129)

During the time of Prophet Hud (peace be upon him), people were wealthy, they were strong and very good at building tall large buildings. Unfortunately, their skills in building was their downfall as they then started to do terible things, like build and sculpt idols. They actually believed in Allah however, they began to worship these idols instead. Prophet Hud tried to warn his people, that worshipping idols was not a good thing to do and that they should worship Allah as He is the only God.

Prophet Hud told them that Allah's punishment would come if they did not listen, and soon enough, there was a drought. There was no rain, trees turned yellow and plants died and the land turned dry.

Then one day a cloud emerged from the sky and people were excited, they expected rain, but instead there was a strong wind that grew stronger and stronger.

(46:25)

So when they saw it as a cloud advancing towards their valleys, they said: "This is just a passing cloud that will bring us rain." No. It is what you were trying to hasten: The wind which carries the grievous punishment! (46: 24)

For seven nights and eight days the wind ripped through their homes, it tore away everything in its way, it destroyed all of their buildings, their sculptures and those who disobeyed and did not believe.

(69: 6-7)

When they saw a cloud approaching their valleys they said,
"This is a cloud that will bring us rain." No, it is rather what
you wanted to speed up : a wind, in which there is a painful
punishment. (46:24)

Prophet Saleh

During Prophet Saleh's time the earth began to shake, the disbelievers were punished with an earthquake.

Prophet Saleh (peace be upon him) was a good man and people at the time relied on him. The Prophet Saleh tried to educate his people about the importance of worshipping Allah (the most amazing, the most high).

Unfortunately, like the generation before them, the people at the time of Prophet Saleh used to worship idols. He would remind them what happened to the people of Prophet Hud (peace be upon him).

(7:59)

The people refused to believe him and told the Prophet Saleh to show them miracles if he was telling the truth.

(11:65)

(7:73)

So Allah then sent down a she-camel as a test, Prophet Saleh told the people to allow the she-camel to eat and live peacefully without harming her. The people did not listen and they killed the she-camel.

(7:77)

Prophet Saleh told his people that they had only three more days to live before Allah would punish them. The people of the city were sorry, but what they did could not be undone, and all those who did not believe were killed in an earthquake. Their city was destroyed and ruined. (26:158)

<u>Holy Quran</u>

Then the earthquake overtook them, so they became motionless bodies in their abode. (7:78)

Prophet Saleh and a few believers who followed him survived.

"We are going to send the she-camel as a trial for them, therefore, watch them and have patience". (54:27)

Prophet Lut

Prophet Lut's people would not listen to Allah, they constantly would stray,

the worst kind of hosts whose guests would never want to stay.

The people during the time of Prophet Lut (peace be upon him) were not good people. The Prophet tried to save them but they were horrible to him and did not believe in him. (7:78)

They did terrible things such as harassing and robbing people who would pass their city, they would always disobey Allah. (29:29)

Allah sent two angels to visit Prophet Lut, they disguised themselves as two men and Prophet Lut began to worry about their safety. He tried to protect them from the people of the city who tried to hurt them.

(11:77)

The angels then revealed their true identities to Prophet Lut, and told him that they had been sent by Allah to;

"..bring down upon the disbelievers a fury from the sky".

(29:34)

Prophet Lut and those who believed in him left the city during the night and were saved, but his wife was a disbeliever and was left behind with the others who did not believe.

(15:59)

When the morning came, God turned the cities upside down, and rained down on them stones hard as baked clay.

(11:82)

Allah sent a punishment of raining giant stones of clay.

A comet shooting from the sky, aimed at those who went astray.

He said: "O my Lord! help Thou me against people who do mischief!" (29:30)

Prophet Ibrahim

Prophet Ibrahim would debate with Nimrod while on his throne he would sit, but he did not listen, as this emporer was a half-wit.

Even as a child, Prophet Ibrahim (peace be upon him) always believed in one God. He never worshipped idols even though his family and friends all did. The Prophet would even try to tell the emperor Nimrod about Allah. Prophet Ibrahim would tell Nimrod, "it is Allah who gives life and death", Nimrod would kill people and say "I too give life and death".

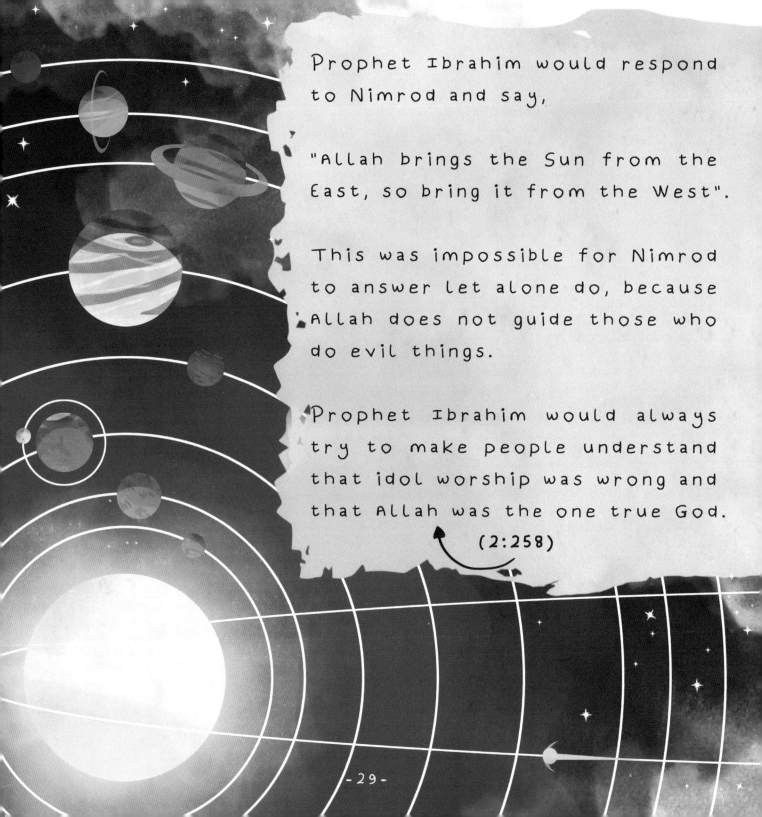

Prophet Ibrahim would respond to Nimrod and say,

"Allah brings the Sun from the East, so bring it from the West".

This was impossible for Nimrod to answer let alone do, because Allah does not guide those who do evil things.

Prophet Ibrahim would always try to make people understand that idol worship was wrong and that Allah was the one true God. (2:258)

He would ask them, "How can you worship what can neither benefit nor harm you, like these idols? Shame on you and on the things you worship instead of Allah."

The idol worshippers were so angry that they decided to punish Prophet Ibrahim by burning him on a bonfire to avenge their Gods.   (21:66-68)

Allah saved Prophet Ibrahim from the fire and it did not harm him.

Holy Quran
"..but we said fire, be cool and safe for Ibrahim." (21:69)

This was one of Prophet Ibrahim's greatest miracles.

Allah said, "O fire, be coolness and safety upon Abraham."

(21:69)

Prophet Ismail

Prophet Ibrahim in the desert had to leave his wife and son, in the scorching heat, under the burning sun.

Prophet Ibrahim continued to teach people about Allah, by now he was an old man and had no children. He wanted children and would pray to Allah to bless him with a child. Allah blessed him with his first son Prophet Ismail (peace be upon him) from his wife Hajar.

(37:101)

Allah revealed to Prophet Ibrahim that he should take his wife Hajar and his baby Prophet Ismail to Makkah, which was a desert at the time. So Prophet Ibrahim took his wife Hajar and his son Prophet Ismail to the desert where there was no food or water.

Before Prophet Ibrahim left them alone, Hajar asked him, "Has Allah told you to do this?" And Prophet Ibrahim replied "Yes".

Hajar then realised that Allah would look after her and Prophet Ismail. It was very difficult for Prophet Ibrahim to leave his baby and his wife, but he had faith in Allah. He prayed towards the Kaaba and asked Allah to look after them. (14:37)

As there was no water and the desert was hot, Hajar and Prophet Ismail began to get very thirsty.

Hajar ran between the Al-Safa and Al-Marwah hills in search of water for her and Prophet Ismail. After the seventh time she ran between the two hills, and an angel then appeared. He helped her and told her that Allah has heard Prophet Ismail crying and that He would provide them with water. That is when Allah caused a spring to burst from the ground, where Prophet Ismail's feet lay.

It was from then onwards that Makkah became known for the water well named Zamzam.

<u>Holy Quran</u>

"O Lord, I have settled some of my descendants in an uncultivated valley near Your sacred House.."
(14:37)

The Sacrifice

When Prophet Ismail grew a little older his dad, Prophet Ibrahim had a dream where he sacrificed his son, he dreamt this many times. Prophet Ibrahim told his son of his dream and Prophet Ismail was ready and willing to do anything to please Allah.

(37:102)

In the Quran it does not mention which son of Prophet Ibrahim was chosen for sacrafice. Some hadiths mention it was Prophet Ismail.

Even though Prophet Ibrahim loved his son very much, he was prepared to do anything for Allah. Prophet Ibraim told Prophet Ismail they had to go to Mount Arafat.

On the way they passed a place called Mina, and that is where Iblis came to Prophet Ibrahim and Ismail. He tried to talk them out of the sacrifice, so they started to throw stones at Iblis. Prophet Ibrahim turned his back on Iblis and would not listen.

When they reached Mount Arafat, Prophet Ibrahim told Prophet Ismail what Allah wanted him to do. Prophet Ismail listened and accepted what was to happen.

Prophet Ismail was such a good person, he put all his trust in Allah and came up with the idea of tying his hands and legs before doing the sacrifice.

Prophet Ismail then told his that his dad to blindfold himself to make it easier to do the sacrifice.

Prophet Ibrahim then took a knife and did what Allah had told him to. When he took the blindfold off he looked down, and realised that it wasn't his son, but a dead ram.

(37:107)

At first Prophet Ibrahim thought he had disobeyed Allah, but then he heard a voice telling him not to worry. Allah looks after his followers.

Prophet Ibrahim and Ismail had passed their test.

Holy Quran

"Indeed, this was the clear trial." (37:106)

After this Prophet Ibrahim and his son Ismail began to rebuild the Kaaba in Makkah. Once they did this they prayed to Allah.

(2:127)

And We ransomed his son with a great sacrifice.

(37:107)

Prophet Ishaq

Prophet Ibrahim had two very special sons,
Prophet Ishaq and Ismail were the chosen ones.

Prophet Ishaq (peace be upon him) is the second son of Prophet Ibrahim. One day angels came to visit Prophet Ibrahim and his wife Sarah, who at the time were too old to have children. The angels came disguised as men, and Prophet Ibrahim invited them into his home to have dinner. The angels did not eat the food, instead they told both Prophet Ibrahim and his wife Sarah that Allah was blessing them with a baby boy named Ishaq, and he would be a Prophet.

(37: 112)

Both of Prophet Ibrahim's sons Ismael and his younger brother Ishaq, were great Prophets whose children went on to teach their people about the oneness of Allah. Prophet Ishaq is the father of Prophet Yaqub.

Holy Quran

"Praise to Allah, who has granted to me in old age Ismail and Ishaq. Indeed, my Lord is the Hearer of supplication." (14:39)

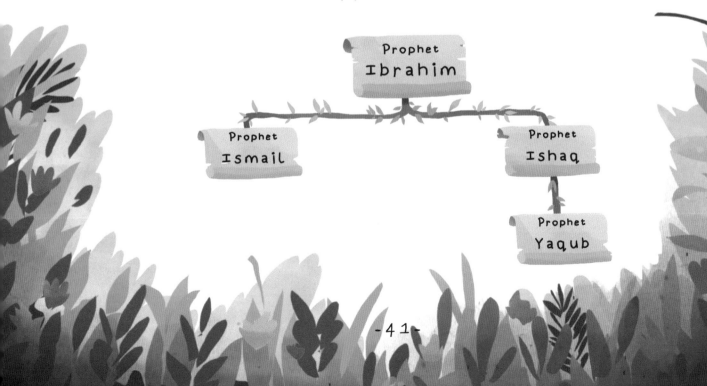

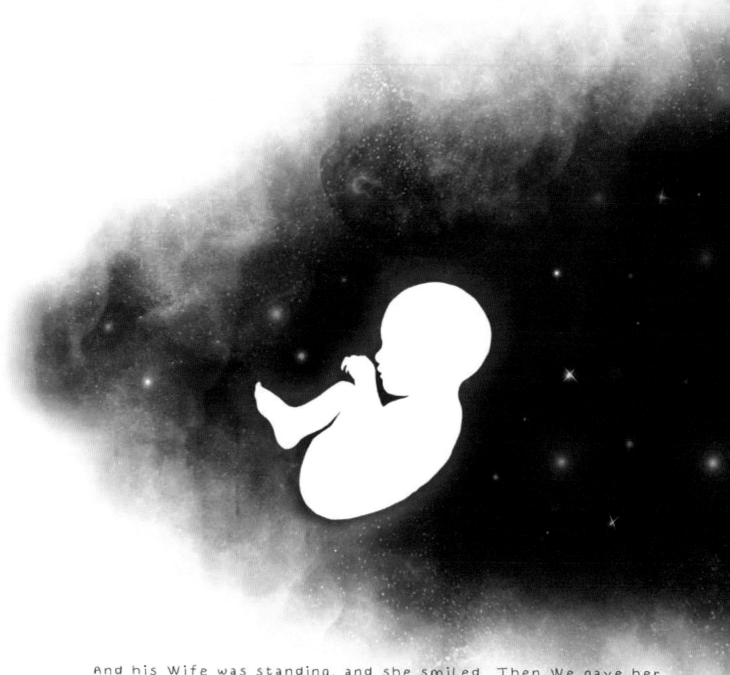

And his wife was standing, and she smiled. Then We gave her good tidings of Ishaq and after Ishaq, Yaqub. (11:17)

And We gave him good tidings of Isaac, a prophet from among the righteous. (37:112)

Prophet Yaqub & Prophet Yusuf

Prophet Yaqub (peace be upon him) was a very good man, he had 12 sons, and one of them was Prophet Yusuf (peace be upon him). One night, Prophet Yusuf went to his dad and told him about a dream that he had.

In his dream he saw stars, planets, the sun and the moon, all of which prostrated towards him.

(2:132)

Prophet Yaqub was Prophet Yusuf's dad, Yusuf was the best son Yaqub had.

The moon and sun prostrated to Yusuf because he was so great, unfortunately his brothers were jealous, their hearts full of hate.

Prophet Yaqub was so happy to hear this because he knew what it meant. He knew that his son Yusuf would become a great Prophet.

Prophet Yaqub's older sons felt that their father loved Yusuf more than them so Prophet Yaqub told Prophet Yusuf not to tell his brothers about his dream. (12:5)

The brothers asked their dad if they could take Yusuf out with them, and promised to look after him.

(2:8-9)

Yusuf's older brothers were very jealous and so they thought of killing Prophet Yusuf, but in the end decided to instead throw him down a well.

(12:15)

The brothers then came home to Prophet Yaqub and pretended to cry, they told their dad a wolf had eaten Prophet Yusuf, and they showed their dad Prophet Yusuf's shirt which they had stained with animal's blood.

(12:18)

Prophet Yaqub knew this was a lie and he always thought about Prophet Yusuf and prayed for him, but he also had faith in Allah's plan. Prophet Yaqub cried so much for Prophet Yusuf that he went blind.

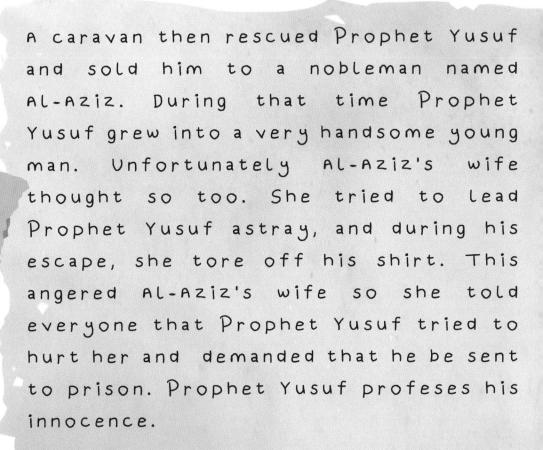

A caravan then rescued Prophet Yusuf and sold him to a nobleman named Al-Aziz. During that time Prophet Yusuf grew into a very handsome young man. Unfortunately Al-Aziz's wife thought so too. She tried to lead Prophet Yusuf astray, and during his escape, she tore off his shirt. This angered Al-Aziz's wife so she told everyone that Prophet Yusuf tried to hurt her and demanded that he be sent to prison. Prophet Yusuf profeses his innocence.

A wise person then explains, "if his shirt is torn from the front, then she has told the truth, and he is a liar but if his shirt is torn from the back, then she has lied, and he is truthful."

(12:27)

They then realise that his shirt is torn from the back, which means he did try to escape. Al-Aziz's wife is embarrassed and the people of the city start to talk about her terrible behaviour. So she decided to hold a dinner party, where all the guests are given fruit cut with knives. While they are cutting their fruit, the wife of Al-Aziz tells Prophet Yusuf to come out. Distracted by his beauty, all the ladies cut their hands, and Al-Aziz's wife tells them not to judge her as they are all as bad as she is. After this she tells Prophet Yusuf that if he does not do what she wants, then she will send him to prison.

(12:32)

Prophet Yusuf went to prison gladly, because he did not want to disobey Allah.

(12:33)

(11:40)

While in prison Prophet Yusuf meets two men who ask him to interpret their dreams. He tells one of the prisoners that his dram means he will be set freeand asks him to tell the King about his special gift of dream interpretation as he knows the King will needthis one day.

Seven years later that king had a dream, he saw seven fat cows eaten by seven thin cows, and seven green crops and seven dry crops. None of the king's advisors knew what this meant. The old prisoner was now working for the King and he remembered what Prophet Yusuf had told him.

Prophet Yusuf was finally allowed to leave the prison to help the king interpret his dream. He told him that the dream meant that Egypt would have seven good years of rain, and healthy crops. After this there would be a drought for seven years and the king would need to save food for the seven years.

As a reward the King requests that Prophet Yusuf be released from prison, the King also investigates his case. It is proven that Prophet Yusuf is innocent and he is rewarded with a high position in Egypt.

(12:55)

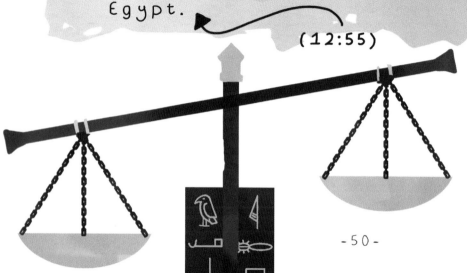

During the terrible drought, Prophet Yusuf's brothers visit Egypt in the hope of getting food for their family. They do not recognise Prophet Yusuf but he recognises them. Prophet Yusuf takes his little brother Benjamin aside and secretly tells him who he is. ◄ (7:69)

Prophet Yusuf then plants something in Benjamin's bag so it looks like he has stolen something, even though he has not. When Benjamin is caught his brothers are forced to leave their little brother behind. They tell Prophet Yaqub what happened and he sends them back to try and get Benjamin back. ◄ (12:88)

They return to try and bring their little brother home and that is when Prophet Yusuf tells his brothers who he is.

(12:90)

He forgives them and gives them his shirt with instructions to wipe it over his father's eyes. The brothers come back with Prophet Yusuf's shirt. Prophet Yaqub's eyesight comes back when he wipes the shirt over his face.

(12:39)

Prophet Yaqub then travels with his sons, and Prophet Yusuf and his family are united again.

And he (Yaqub pbuh) said, "Oh, my sorrow over Yusuf," and his eyes became white from grief because of the sorrow that he suppressed. (12:84)

Prophet Musa

Firawn did not know it yet but the messenger Musa was on his way, this obviously meant that Firawn most definitely could not stay.

Before Prophet Musa (peace be upon him) was born, there were lots of problems between the Egyptians and the Israelites. To make matters worse, there was a terrible ruler who ruled over Egypt and treated the Israelites very badly, his name was Firawn. One night Firawn had a dream, and he told his advisor. His interpretation was that a baby boy from the Israelites would be born and would free all the slaves and kill him.

Holy Quran

"..for he was indeed a maker of mischief" (28:4)

So Firawn thought of a terrible plan, he would kill all the baby boys born to the Israelites so that he could stop his dream from coming true.

Prophet Musa was one of those babies, so his mother decided to keep her pregnancy secret. When Prophet Musa was born his mother and little sister put him in a basket and placed him in a river.

(28:7)

They prayed to Allah to look after the baby, and Prophet Musa's sister followed the basket and watched as it drifted to Firawn's palace.

Firawn's wife Asiya saw the baby and she knew that he was an Israelite. She persuaded Firawn to keep the baby and to raise him as their own, even though he wanted to kill him, in the end Firawn accepted. (28:9)

Prophet Musa would cry and cry and every time they tried to get him a wet nurse to feed him, he wouldn't feed. He was miserable, it wasn't until his mother came to the palace to offer her help that Prophet Musa finally stopped crying and would happily be fed. (28:13)

Prophet Musa grew up in Firawn's home and it wasn't until years had passed and he grew older, that he knew how difficult life was in Egypt, especially for an Israelite. This is when Prophet Musa saw a fire and approached it.

Holy Quran

But when he came to the (Fire), a voice was heard from the right bank of the valley, from a tree in hallowed ground: "O Moses! Verily I am Allah the Lord of the Worlds..." (28:30)

This was the beginning of Prophet Musa's mission and his prophethood.

Prophet Musa had two things to do, save the Israelites from Firawn, and tell the Egyptians to worship Allah alone and to be better people. He showed Firawn the miracles from Allah by turning his staff into a snake, and a light would shine from his hand.   (27:12)

But Firawn did not believe and called Prophet Musa a magician.

In the end Prophet Musa saved the Israelites by rescuing them and splitting the sea.

(26:63)

Firawn was close behind them trying to catch and attack Prophet Musa and the Israelites. Prophet Musa prayed to Allah and split the sea with his staff, all the Israelites crossed to the other side. As Firawn ran into the sea, he and his followers all drowned as the split sea crashed into them.

We inspired Moses' mother, saying, 'Suckle him, and then, when you fear for his safety, put him in the river: do not be afraid, and do not grieve, for We shall return him to you and make him a messenger.' (28:7)

And when We saved your forefathers from the people of Pharaoh, who afflicted you with the worst torment, slaughtering your (newborn) sons and keeping your females alive. And in that was a great trial from your Lord. (2:49)

Prophet Sulayman

Prophet Sulayman had many special gifts and was the most powerful of kings, he could speak to jinns and all kinds of animals, even ones with wings.

Prophet Sulayman (peace be upon him) was a very powerful man, Allah gave him the gift of speaking to animals and Jinn. He was grateful to Allah for all his gifts and he always tried to serve Allah.

Prophet Sulayman had an army of not only men but Jinns and animals too. One day Prophet Sulayman was marching with his army of different creatures, and on his way he saw a small group of ants going about their business.

Holy Quran

And Sulaiman was Dawood's heir, and
he said: O men! We have been taught
the language of birds, and we have
been given all things; most surely
this is manifest grace. (27:16)

When the ants saw Prophet Sulayman approaching with his army, one of them yelled,

"Quick, let's hide and get out of the way before Prophet Sulayman and his army crush us, because they may not see us".

Prophet Sulayman smiled, because he heard and knew what the ants had said because Allah gave him the gift of understanding animals and insects.

Holy Quran

And there were gathered before Sulayman his hosts of jinns and men, and birds, and they all were set in battle order (marching forwards).

Till, when they came to the valley of the ants, one of the ants said: "O ants! Enter your dwellings, lest Sulayman and his hosts crush you, while they perceive not." (27: 17-18)

Prophet Yunus

Poor Prophet Yunus had no patience for his people, so for the sea he set sail, but Allah had other plans for him and he was eaten by a whale.

Prophet Yunus (peace be upon him) was sent by Allah to the people of Nineveh. It was a great city but unfortunately, it had become a place full of terrible people. Prophet Yunus told the people to turn to Allah and be better, but they did not listen and he grew tired of them. Prophet Yunus couldn't help but give up on his people and he decided to leave.

He then boarded a ship to get as far away as possible.

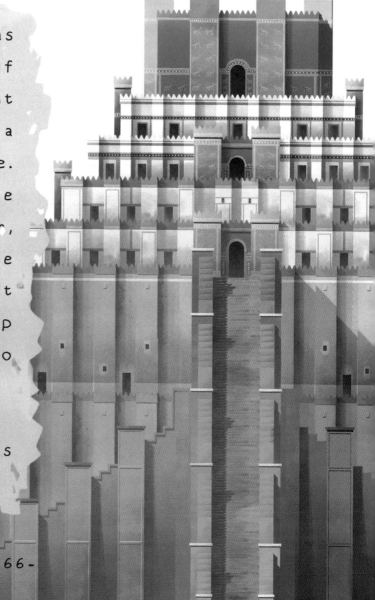

Once he set off sail, a storm began and the crew were terrified. The Pagan sailors feared that their Gods were unhappy with them. They decided to draw lots to determine who should be thrown overboard as a sacrifice, they did this three times and each time Prophet Yunus was chosen to be thrown overboard.

The pagans threw Prophet Yunus overboard in the hope that it would protect them and the ship. That is when something extraordinary happened, Allah sent a huge whale to swallow Prophet Yunus whole.

Prophet Yunus was in the belly of the whale and he was scared and worried. He was trapped in total darkness.

Holy Quran

"He cried through the darkness." (21:87)

Prophet Yunus realised that he no longer had control of anything, and that Allah was the one who was in control of what would happen to him. Prophet Yunus prayed to Allah for help and that is when something wonderful happened. The whale spat out Prophet Yunus whole onto land and he was saved.

After everything he had gone through, poor Prophet Yunus started to feel sick and weak, as he lay on the sand in the scorching heat, Allah helped him once again by making a plant grow over him to give him shade from the burning sun.

Once he felt better he then went back to his people in Nineveh, and to his surprise everyone had become good and now they worshiped Allah.

Maryam & Prophet Isa

Maryam (peace be upon her) was the mother of Prophet Isa (peace be upon him) and his birth was like no other birth, it was a miracle. When Maryam realised she was expecting a child, she was very confused.

Holy Quran

"She said, 'My Lord, how will I have a child when no man has touched me?' (The angel) said, 'Such is Allah; He creates what He wills. When He decrees a matter, He only says to it, "Be," and it is.'" (3:47)

Maryam devoted herself to Allah. She hid herself from everyone, and gave birth to Prophet Isa under a date palm tree. Under that same tree is where dates dropped down which is what she ate to help her during Prophet Isa's birth.

When she returned to her village with Prophet Isa in her hands. The villagers were shocked and began to say bad things about her, they thought she must have sinned as she had a baby and was not married.

Maryam was strong and had so much faith in Allah. Allah always helped Maryam, He had given Prophet Isa the gift of performing miracles.

One of the miracles Allah gave Prophet Isa was the ability to speak as a baby, this not only shocked everyone but confirmed Maryam was telling the truth.

Not only could Prophet Isa speak as a baby, but he was able to perform other miracles too.

(3:49)

Prophet Isa on many occasions would tell his people that he was a messenger and not the son of Allah.

(4:171-172)

After many years Prophet Isa was raised to the heavens and not crucified on a cross.

Holy Quran

"And they said, "Indeed, we have killed the Messiah, Jesus, son of Maryam, the messenger of Allah." But they did not kill him, nor did they crucify him; but (another) was made to resemble him.." (4:157)

Prophet Muhammad

Prophet Muhammad is the last of all the messengers and he always told the truth. He brought the Holy Quran with all it's miracles as proof.

The Holy Prophet Muhammad (peace be upon him) was an amazing person, and Allah sent him as the last Prophet with the message of Islam. This was the same message as previous Prophets had brought.

(68:4)

(39:33)

One day Prophet Muhammad was retreating in a cave called Hira, which is near Mecca. That was when the angel Gabriel came to him and told him to recite the following verse:

Holy Quran

"Read in the name of your Lord who created you.."

(96.1)

The Holy Prophet Muhammad then went home and told his wife Khadijah about what happened and she believed him. She was the first person to become a Muslim and she helped the Holy Prophet to teach people about Islam.

Prophet Muhammad brought the Holy Quran and taught people to believe in one God (Allah). He also taught other things such as, showing women respect, caring for your parents and treating people fairly and with kindness.

(4:19)   (2:163)   (17:23)

There were many people who were part of the Quraysh tribe who disbelieved and disobeyed Allah and his Prophet. Even the holy Prophet's own Uncle hated him, and wanted him dead. So in the night the holy Prophet and his companion fled to a cave.

When the Quraysh reached the opening of the cave, the holy Prophet turned to his companion (with utmost trust in Allah and no worry at all) he said, "Do not grieve. Allah is surely with us." As the Quraysh passed the cave they did not suspect a thing. The Holy Prophet Muhammad was the final prophet Allah sent and he brought us the holy Qur'an.

(9:40)

"And We certainly sent into every nation a messenger, (saying), "Worship Allah and avoid Taghut." And among them were those whom Allah guided, and among them were those upon whom error was (deservedly) decreed.
(Quran, 16:36)

Printed in Great Britain
by Amazon

20788666R00045